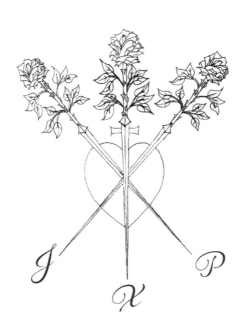

Published by Mater Media
St. Louis, Missouri
www.matermedia.org

Cover and Interior Design: Trese Gloriod • DesignproChristus.com

978-1-7365190-9-7

Passion Flowers in Bloom

Hailey Kathleen Hall

MATER
MEDIA

Foreword by the Author

The book you hold in your hand is the fruit of my five years spent discerning a possible call to the life of a cloistered contemplative in a Passionist Monastery in Ellisville, Missouri. During these five years of prayer and penance, I was immersed in the "Memoria Passionis" (Memory of the Passion), the charism of the Passionist Congregation. When I entered the novitiate, I was given the name "Sister Isidora Maria of the Holy Will of God," a name chosen to honor Blessed Isidore de Loor, a Passionist brother who shared my desire to always follow God's Holy Will. It was this focus on the Passion, Christ's incredible, ineffable, and incomprehensible act of love for my soul, that led me into the cloister... and out again.

In Autumn of 2020, after much discernment, prayer, (and heartache) I realized that God was calling me to a different life, and, in my never-ending desire to better follow the Holy Will of God, I embraced His call and left the cloister to start a new life in St. Louis, far from home and family. My trust in Him was rapidly rewarded a hundred fold... Three days after I left the enclosure, I met Michael in front of the chapel, and a year later, on October 2nd, 2021, we were joined as one in the Sacrament of Holy Matrimony. How Providence arranged that meeting is a story that requires more space than allotted for this foreword, but suffice it to say, I am grateful for every moment I spent in the convent. It made me who I am today.

I wrote Passion Flowers as a way to promote the Memoria Passionis, a way of deepening the appreciation of the Passion in the hearts of all, and that intention still stands. I am still on very good terms with the Passionist Nuns in Ellisville, and when Mater Media expressed interest in publishing Passion Flowers, they not only gave their permission for this endeavor, but their blessing as well. With the blessing of my husband and the publisher, I have arranged that the proceeds from the sale of this book will be given to them.

I pray that what you encounter in these pages will draw you closer to the foot of the Cross and bring you deeper into the Wounds of Love!

May the Passion of our Lord Jesus Christ
Be Ever in Our Hearts

Mrs. Hailey Hall

List of Poems

List of Illustrations

Enclosed

Within Cloister Walls,
In Hallowed Halls,
Pervaded by Silence Sweet,

Can be heard the Rustle Soft
Of Habits aloft
Above Be-Sandaled Feet.

Rosaries jingle Sweetly
Swinging so Neatly
From the Belt of Each and all,

And the Veils of Black
flow down the Back
The same, no matter How Tall

With a nod and smile
as we pass Single File
Many times throughout the Day

Prayer in each heart
Sets us Apart
And unites us in a Way

For though we are
from near and far
we are Sisters all the same

Our hearts are one
as we love the Son
For t'was He who called us by name

Forever to Stand
with heart in Hand
with the Church, His Virgin Bride

And so we remain
ever the same
Doves of the Crucified

The Voice

I heard a Voice, begging my choice
"Will you serve your Love, Who reigns in Heaven above?"
Would I give all that I possess, all hope of worldly success
to serve Him alone, for sins of men to atone?
All that was mine, would vanish in time,
power, prestige, wealth…success, honor, health…
Would I give it all up, could I drink the Cup?
What a choice to make, my whole life at stake
Could I leave the world's many frills and curls
and cling to the rock, the fruit of David's Stock?
How can the world compare, to Him, the Fairest of Fair
Him of the Thorny Crown, in whose Love I could Drown?
Him of Glory, Power, and Might, who comes like a thief in the night
How could I dare resist, Him upon whom I subsist?
He upon Whom I daily feed, Who fulfills my every want or need?
And so I say to the voice, "you already know my choice,
for you know the depths of my heart, and though I know not where to start,
I know what I shall do, I give my all to You!"
I hear joy in His Voice as I make my choice:
"Then come to me, my love, fly home my little dove!"
Home? Where could it be? I know not, I cannot see,
the path that lies ahead, upon which my feet tread
is shrouded in mist so thick, and overgrown with thorns that prick
"Lord, show me the way! Turn my dark into day!
Like fire, the Light drives away the night
Now my eyes are open, all the shame has fallen
like scales from my eyes, and all is clear blue skies
Lord, the Path is far from wide, and danger lurks on every side
but my feet tread swift and true, as I make my way to You
keep me safe on the journey, Love, as I come to You in heaven above.

Ode to the Creator

In the Summer Breeze, The Starlit Sky
The Firefly that passes by.
In the Rain, in the Storm,
In the Clouds and the Shapes they form.
In the Dusk, at the Dawn,
In a newborn Foal or Fawn.
In the Tide as it ebbs,
In the Dew on Spider's Webs
Everywhere I look I see,
Little things that prove to me
That God Is Present, He is real
He made all I see and feel.
He made the Grass, the Trees, the Sky,
The colors of a Butterfly.
He sends the Rain, He moves the Wind,
And nurtures the Garden that I tend.
And most of all, I dare to say,
He is my Bread of the Day.
I partake of Him every Morn
Rain or Shine, Snow or Storm.
He is my Life, He is my Love,
Him who comes from Heav'n above.
Never may I forget Thee Lord,
Nor treasure on this Earth to Hoard,
For I long to reach my Heavenly Home
Far above this Earthly Dome.
Oh My Love, may I reside,
Within Thy Heart in thy piercéd side,
And by Thy Blood be washed of Stain,
So that with Thee I may ever remain.

Passion Flower

Little Flower Smelling Sweet
I dare not show to all I meet

So beautiful, this rose blood-red
upon whose petals I am fed.

Grown in soil oh so rich
watered with Blood, dark as pitch.

Passion flowers grow so strong
in His side where they belong.

Like little Doves they coo and cry
with tears of mourning that never dry

For sorrow overwhelms hearts so meek
who for their Beloved ever seek.

They have seen Him bruised and beaten
and of His flesh they have eaten

They moan and cry with hearts aflame,
when they hear Him call by name

His little Brides, O' Virgins all
who are ever at His beck and call.

With lamps alight they await
the Bridegroom, their most Holy Date.

He meets them at death's dark door
He whom they forever waited for.

He calls to them and bids them "Come,"
to Him in the heavenly kingdom

Where they shall evermore reside
never to be parted from His side.

A Passion Flower's one true quest
is to be the Lamb's Wedding Guest.

Their only aim, their Eternal Goal
is to be united as One Soul

to their Heavenly Spouse, their King
and forevermore His praises Sing.

For they are prudent and most wise
and with the world have severed ties.

They live lives of sweet serenity
as they long await Eternity.

These are Flowers of the Passion True
akin to Doves that mournfully coo

Who, enclosed within His Heart and Side
shall always and evermore reside.

Little Dove

Oh little dove you moan and cry
For thy Love the Lord Most High
In the crook of His mighty Arm
You He took safe from harm
For at His power His strength and Might
Demons cower flee in the night
But you are safe for He took you in
Like a waif safe to His den
You He protects from Satan's lies
The Lion rejects the Serpent's guise
He tries to deceive you whom Christ loves
To make you leave be no more His Doves
Birds of Prey he wants you to be
But you will stay you know, you see
That he is the liar this "angel of light"
Who stokes Hell's fire in the dead of night
So cling close to the Side of your One True Love
For you are His Bride His sweet little Dove.

Creation's Song

I thank Thee Lord for giving me
ears to hear and eyes to see
words of Truth and Life and Grace
and glorious Visions of Thy Face
I thank Thee too, for a tongue to taste
and fingers to feel, not a thing to waste
All are from Thee, these gifts of Thine
these little sharings in the Life Divine
Gazing in wonder at a star-lit sky
what Glory revealed to the human eye
and even in the dark of night
there is such beauty and such light
in the song of the crickets, the hoot of an owl
the croak of a toad and the wolf's lone howl
All reveal that Thou art their King
of Thee they speak, to Thee they sing
Creation's Song praises Thy Word
Thou its origin, Thou its Lord
Father-Creator, Redeemer-Son
Spirit of Fire, Thou Three-in-one
have given creation as Man's domain
of which to protect, over which to reign
Let us not squander, nor waste and destroy
for the earth is God's Gift, and not Man's toy

Lent

With violet sashes
and palm frond ashes
we know that Lent has arrived
That time of fasting
can seem long lasting
as we dine on fish that's fried.
Yes, truth be told,
it can get old
and forty days may seem a long time
But it's not all bad,
there's more to be had
than just the Ash Wednesday line
Giving up treats,
eating less sweets
may seem the right thing to do
Noble we feel at first,
yet soon, parched with thirst,
we may longingly look at the brew.
As the end looks so far,
how tempted we are
to rush on past that Friday-Good
But it would be to our loss
to ignore the Cross
and despise its blood-stained wood.
For, with penance and prayer
we become more aware
of how much we owe our Lord:
For t'was for us that He died,
was mocked, scourged, crucified
and His Mother's Heart pierced by the Sword.

Fall

I fall to my knees
in Autumn's crisp breeze
my face warmed by the Sun

How can I not
adore in this spot
the Uncreated One?

He made the leaves
that dance on the trees
in dresses of red and gold

the harvest moon's light
and the starlit night
proclaim "He made us of old"

Bonfires burn
as my heart and soul yearn
to be set ablaze by His love

and be turned all to flame
when He calls my name
to join Him in the Heavens above

as I fall to my knees
in the crisp fall breeze
my tongue bursts forth in song

and as Autumn leaves fall
in love I call
"O Beloved Lord, How long?"

The Magdalene

What lies beneath the Wench's guise
heart of a thief, a life of lies
how can it be, does she not know
she's been set free, from grip of foe
Her Beloved has died to give her life
she's no longer to hide for he bore her strife
He took the whip, the nails and thorn
every kiss of her lip, every sin he's borne
Rejoice O' Mary, your devils have gone
Now, do not tarry, over men to fawn
but rush to the one to whom you belong
run to the Son sing him your love song
Healed, Restored, Renewed, Forgiven
No more to be whored, no more forsaken
for our Beloved has paid the price for you and I
let us do as He's bade and join him in the sky!

Longinus' Lament

Here in my hand I can feel the weight
with my knees in the sand and my heart wrapt in hate
of hammer and nail, of mallet and stake
Though I cannot fail to pity the fake
who said He was king, not that it matters to me
"hail Caesar" I sing (for I'm a Roman, you see)
Then why does it ache, down so deep in my soul
I'm to drive in the stake, yet I tremble like a foal
In His eyes, those eyes! Someone cover them please!
I see my sins, my lies! Break the gaze, make him cease
to look with such compassion on my wretched sinful soul
any blindfold I could fashion cannot cover the hole
that He bore in my heart, with that look, with that Love
How can I now play my part, and murder Him from Heav'n above?
Yet I know that I must do exactly as I was told
for though Innocent and Just, He was far too bold
If only He'd not said such wondrous words
of that Kingdom He'd bought without shields or swords
maybe then they would just have left Him alone
but then how could He for their sins atone?
As my muscles tense, and I raise the hammer high
I know He can sense that His earthly end is nigh
I watch His face as I swing hard and strong
Through the pain, the Grace, the Love remains all along
The hammer strikes thrice to drive in each nail
as my friends cast dice, how can they not fail
to cringe when they hear each sharp metallic clang
as my eyes begin to tear for I know that He'll soon hang
and shall die for all our sin, for to us he spoke to
when he said "Father forgive them for they know not what they do."

14

Litany

blood sweat tears
Death, as Man, God fears
As You Will, so let it be

Peter James John
asleep upon the lawn
Arise! they come for me

torch club sword
all fall at His word
I AM the one ye seek

silent dumb still
led to temple hill
the Lamb, gentle, meek

elder priest scribe
all condemn to die
God's Son He claims to be

innocent just true
"what evil did he do?"
Pilate: "Scourge then free"

pillar chain thong
bound by Romans strong
the scourge, a thing of dread

rip gouge tear
blood flies through the air
His Flesh torn and shred

King? soldiers glee
bow on bended knee
oh thorn, the perfect crown

cloak crown reed
now before crowd lead
Behold, thy King! a clown

priests mob men
Christ, away they send
Barabbas, he they choose

hands water rinse
Pilate's movements tense
Caesar as friend he'll lose

Pilate judge seat
his one remembered feat
Jesus, condemned to die

robbers one two
hands bound to crosses too
but Christ, no need to tie.

thorns piercing head
through crowded town led
the Cross on shoulder borne

Mother Son meet
a look so tender, sweet
their hearts with sorrow torn

trip stumble fall
Simon the Cyrenean call
help sent from above

cloth wipe face
an act, so full of grace
the Veil, an Icon of Love

hot sun daze
blinded by dusty haze
He falls hard upon knee

women weep wail
Jesus stops to hail
Daughter Zion, weep not for me

tunic vesture strip
wounds freshly drip
His Robe, for lots, cast

hands feet pierce
the pain intense and fierce
His Throne embraced at last

Satan play hand
darkness covers the land
The Son, His life now lost

rocks veil rent
new life to dead lent
the Christ, dead on the Cross

women mourn weep
Guards, watch now keep
the Body in tomb laid

night come quick
light the Sabbath wick
The Lord asleep in grave

new dawn break
to tomb spices take
Empty! How can it be?

angels cloth stone
"He is risen, He alone!"
He's gone to Galilee

Peter John run
make for rising sun
It's true! We can see!

Lord God King
Let all creation sing
Alleluia! We are free!!

Tell us Longinus

Tell us Longinus, of Him Nailed to the Wood
Tell us, oh tell us, of that Friday called Good
Tell us of Hammer, Tell us of Nail
Tell us how Roman's aim did not fail
Tell us of casting lots for His Clothes
and tell us, oh tell us how you won His Robe
Tell us Longinus of the watch and the wait
as High Priest and Levite spouted lies and hate
Tell us of Dismas and how he turned from his way
and tell us of Mary who by the Cross did stay
Tell us Longinus of His unquenchable Thirst
of His pains and His agonies, which was the worst?
Tell us, oh Roman, of early come night
as sun hid its face from the horrible sight
Tell us of how it was at the end
when His soul to His Father He deigned to commend
Tell us, Oh tell us! for we long to know:
how it felt to deliver that last fated blow
O tell us Longinus, tell us it all
His Life and His death, every Cross-laden fall
Tell us that we too may come to believe
in the Blood and the Water that made Your eyes see
Tell us Longinus! Please tell us the tale
of how you were saved through Hammer and Nail

17

Sunrise

At the Dawn the rising Sun
colors the sky, a gift from the One
The Master Artist, with Brush in hand
paints the sky, the trees, the land
Purples and pinks, greens and blues
no man could imagine such incredible hues
With strong strokes, crisp clear lines are formed
and with a softer touch the clouds are born
Man, try as he might cannot recreate
all that beauty, he can but imitate
for there is no artist that, on earth, can compare
to Him who created the Glory of Earth's fare
What can Man do when in awe the Earth behold
but give glory to Him of Whom it is told
that He made the Earth and formed the lands
as a potter molds clay, deftly in His hands
What an Artist is He who formed all we see
our praise to Him is due, who made you and me
So sing of the beauty of the rising Sun
as you partake of His Glory, the Mighty Three-in-One

19

Season's End

As the Season draws to a close,
we remember not Rudolph's nose
nor the sound of "Jingle Bells"
nor gingerbread and how it smells
Frosty has become a puddle
and the world is not so subtle
as the candy and hearts all seem to say
"Now it's on to the next holiday!"
Trees and lights have come down fast
but we shall not just hurry past
we shall draw near the manger wood
and recall that of the Friday-Good
when that Babe, just born for you and I
upon the Cross did suffer and die
For without the Death of Mary's little Son
our Freedom, our Glory could not have been won
As the Passionist Nuns are oft to say
no matter what the Holy-Day,
"May the Passion of Christ whom the Angels adore,
be sealed on your hearts, now and forever more!"

Horarium

There is a pattern
to the life I lead
with time to learn
and time to read
there are times to pray
and days to fast
and though each day
may be similar to the last
it does not bore me
this life of mine
but sets me free
to find the Divine
Strict as though
the schedule may seem
it serves a goal
it meets a need
for time is a gift
from Heav'n above
so my heart can lift
to Him Whom I love!

How Long?

How long must I wear this bridal veil,
oh when will that day come
when upon the ocean of Thy Love I sail
and our two hearts be made One?
How long must I wear my wedding gown
how long till Thou makest me Thine
When Thou shalt take me as Thy Own
and say of my soul: "Thou art Mine"?
How long, O' Lord, must I await
that all consuming Fire
those flames of Love, O glorious Fate
of which I could never tire?
How long, my King, must my heart yearn
to be One, my Love, with Thee
shall night to day forever turn
and Thy face I never see?
How Long, O' Beloved of my soul
my God, my Lord, my King
till Thou shalt fill that God-Shaped Hole
and make my full heart sing?
How Long, I cry, my heart it breaks
with longing so deep and strong
I weary of the time it takes
as I sing this mournful song!
How Long till the nights of waiting end
and the days stop dragging on
Oh when shall I to Thee ascend
O' Jesus, my Love, How long?

Littleness

Lord, I don't know what I'm doing,
I don't know why I'm here:

Why is it I'm not praying?
What is it that I fear?

I'm afraid of dying,
I'm afraid of leaving here.

But that's not it, not all-
of what I'm most afraid

is that my heart's too small
to hold What's in it laid.

My heart, so small and broken
how can it hold within

the Word to mankind spoken
when we were dead in sin?

How can He Who made sea and sky
and formed the earthen land;

Who taught the Doves to fly,
and showed men how to stand;

How can He, the Lord of all,
the King of Time and Space

fit in a heart so small,
In such a tiny place?

and yet, somehow He's there,
for though I feel Him not

In my soul I am aware
that He loves the lowly spot!

And though I feel apart,
because of Sin and Pride,

He's there within my heart
and loves me as His Bride!

Water and Wheat

Water and wheat and wine that's sweet
now hands have blest and broken
Neither sight nor smell, nor taste can tell
change wrought by the words then spoken
But where once was bread and wine blood red
lies a gift more precious than gold
For in Faith's light clear, with awe and fear
'tis our God we now behold.
Our Father in Heaven has supplied the leaven,
His Son with the thorn-crowned head.
Strange as it may seem, this is what we mean
when we pray for our Daily Bread.
So Christian true come pay your due
to Christ whom Death did know
and receive Him not with stain or spot
but pure as wind-driven snow
Once cleansed of sin, receive Him in
to your heart where He may reside
and beg the grace to see His face
and live in His piercéd side
O' Jesus the Son, with the Father, one
and Spirit, life giving flame
Come to my heart and set it apart
that it may crave more of the same
of this Water and Wheat and that Wine, so sweet
that Hands have blest and broken
for though sight nor smell, nor taste can tell,
I believe in the Words then spoken!

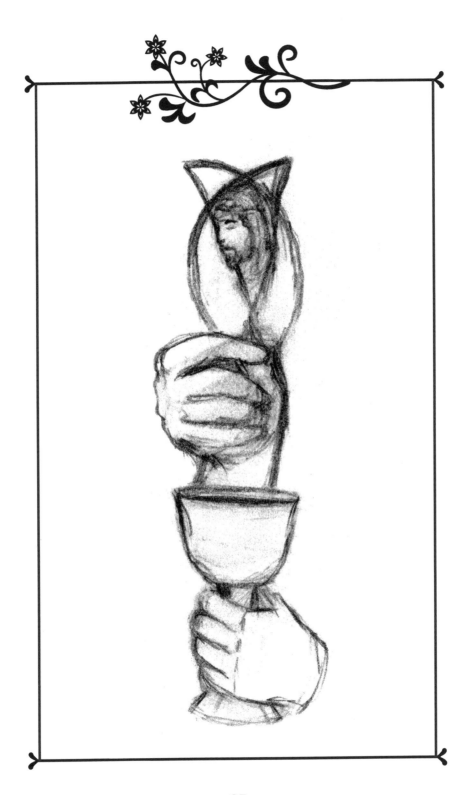

Molded

O Lord my God, I know that You are there
as I scream and cry and tear out my hair

So why don't I hear your answer-
I know that You can see

that I really need Your help,
Please Lord, answer me!

I grit my teeth in anger
as I scream silent screams:

"Lord, this ain't easy!
It's much harder than it seems!"

I do what I don't want to,
I don't do what I ought,

O Lord, make haste and help me-
Make me what I'm not!

Patience is a virtue
I'm afraid I don't possess

and Temperance demands
that my plate be piled less;

My curiosity, it kills me
as my eyes rove all around

why must it be so hard
to keep them modestly cast down?

They say "Silence is Golden"
and our rule prescribes it too,

but when I know I should shut up
I find it hard to do!

Lord, though I may not hear Your Voice,
I know You hear my prayer,

'Cause no matter where I look,
Your prints are everywhere:

You help me increase in Virtue
You keep me from all Vice

You give me many Graces
so that Sin does not entice.

You know this life ain't easy
that's why each and every day

Your Hands, they shape and mold me,
for I am very stubborn clay!

Bleeding Heart

He feels the warmth seeping,
cooling as it drips
as He tries to speak
through His cracked, dry-parched lips
"Eloi! Eloi!"
His voice rings out clear,
"Lema sabachthani!"
Loud enough for all to hear
"My God!, My God!"
so the translation goes,
His Heart, It breaks
The words His agony shows
Body beaten, bruised, bloody
His limbs nailed to a tree
His Blood gushed forth in torrents
to set all mankind free
O how can we repay Him
for all the Blood He shed
When we let ourselves each day
be further from Him led?
Like those weary travelers
so many years ago
we all have too much business
and many a place to go.
Let us not be like them
who looked, but did not see
Him Whose Blood was poured out
for sinners like you and me
Let us stay a while
Beneath His piercéd side
and let that Torrent flow over us
to be cleansed by Its Blood-red Tide.

Follow the Lamb

Follow the Lamb
wherever He goes
whether obscured by night
or wind-driven snows.
In times of pain,
in deepest sorrow,
though it may seem
there'll be no morrow,
just look to the Cross
and you will see
how much He went through
for you and for me.
Let His suffering and pain,
His anguish and strife,
breathe new strength to your soul
and give you new life
For t'was through His Agony
His Death on the Cross
that we were Redeemed
He paid our cost.
So rejoice and be glad
for in pain one knows
that we're truly following the Lamb
wherever He goes.

Mary Sleeps

With Her Last Life's-Breath
She sleeps in death
and on Earth no tears are shed
Mary's sleeping
is not time for weeping
we sing Hymns of praise instead
Dear sweet Mary
did not tarry
for long in an earthen grave
She was raised aloft
on clouds so soft
by Her Son Who died to Save
When Mary slept
the Apostles leapt
their hearts with gladness ring
From the Earth asleep
on High She'd leap
and with Joy make the Heavens ring
When our death looms nigh
at our last sigh
and we must exit this earthly stage
Then let us adore
what waits in store
for us at the end of the age
When death we embrace
tears, do not waste
for someday we shall arise
and whence Mary went
we too shall be sent:
Our Heavenly Home in the skies!

Septenary

Seven days of Penance
Seven days of Prayer
This little that I offer
seems like more than I can bear
In Honor of His Mother
as beneath the Cross She stands
I kneel with arms outstretched
as if the Nails were in my hands
Seven times: "Our Father"
Seven times: "Hail Full-of-Grace"
As thoughts of Mary's Sorrow
make tears roll down my face
Oh Dear Sweet Mary
what pain you must've felt
As that Sword of sorrow
was thrust unto the hilt
All that I have to offer
now seems like so much sand
how I wish there were more
that I could place into His hand!
Seven days of Penance
Seven Days of Prayer
This little that I suffer
is it all that I can bear?

34

The Dove

The master came to walk the lane
amidst the morning dew
He looked around: the lily abound
and roses, blood-red too
With scent so sweet around His feet
I thought that He would stay
Yet He stooped not in beauty's spot
but continued on His way
He came abreast of my nest
my little thistle bed
When He looked down I thought He'd frown
He smiled with love instead
Through thorny prick His hand did stick
and plucked me from my home
And held me aloft in hands so soft
and claimed me as His own
How can it be? Why choose me
and clutch me to His Side?
How little and weak is the one He seeks
and calls to be His bride!
Oh King of Kings, To You I sing
to You I pay my Vows
I am Your Dove, O Jesus my Love
To whom I am Espoused!

Wedding Feast

It was a party, a true wedding feast
with many invited, the greatest and least.
The men were a-dancing, swaying to and fro
at Cana in Galilee, so long, long ago.

One could be noted, apart from the rest
He danced with abandon, this joyous Wedding Guest
He danced and He swayed, back and forth, to and fro
at Cana in Galilee, so long, long ago.

He sang as He danced in a tenor crystal clear
with joyous delight, a wonder to hear
He sang of the Blessing that God did bestow
at Cana in Galilee, so long, long ago.

The guests rejoiced at the sound of His song
as He gained in momentum they all sang along
He let them take over, dropped His voice down low
at Cana in Galilee, so long, long ago.

He stole away as the song reached its peak
for there was His mother, waiting to speak.
"There is no more wine." Her voice soft and low
at Cana in Galilee, so long, long ago.

He looked at His Mother with no real surprise
"Woman" He says, with love in His eyes
What you ask, it means, you already know…
at Cana in Galilee, so long, long ago.

With trusting love, she turns from her Son
and beckons the servants, who come, one by one.
"Whatever He tells you, do as you're told"
at Cana in Galilee, so long, long ago.

At His mother's request, He performed His first sign
which foreshadowed His last, this water made wine
The first of His miracles, Jesus did show
at Cana in Galilee, so long, long ago.

Through the intercession of Mary, God changed His plan
and hastened redemption for woman and man
Those five small words held so much in tow
at Cana in Galilee, so long, long ago.

Rather sooner than later when at the Cross she'd stand
looking up at her Son, nailed feet and hand
She'd remember the day she let her Son go…
at Cana in Galilee, so long, long ago.

Snowsong

The flakes of white in winter seen
fall so soft in silence supreme
all is hush there is no sound
to break the peace that doth abound
nary a bird wings thru the sky
or sings out its song or lets loose it's cry
yes, all is quiet, all is still
in time of cold and frost and chill
yet in the silence in winter's hush
there is a music beautifully lush
not to be heard with bodily ears
nor by those tightly wound by fears
but still the soul quiet the mind
open the heart and one may find
the sound in the silence oh so deep
of choirs of angels singing Jesus to sleep.
Peace on Earth to all men of good will
may you rest in that silence so soft and so still
and as your heart basks in that Starlight
sing to your Savior born this night.

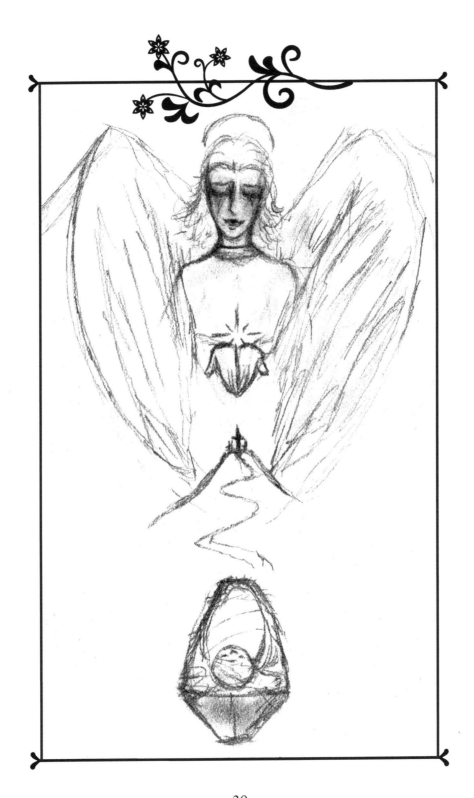

40

Agony

Before You in prayer, supplication for grace
I plead with You, Father, hide not Your face
The Cup, the Chalice, please make it pass
the pain, the agony let it not last
Oh Abba! Oh Father! Must it be so?
Must I, Your Son, to the Cross now go?
Yet, Abba! Dear Father, I am Your Son
Thy will, not mine, let it be done.
Your hand is heavy, take it from me
The evil, the sin! It's all I can see.
The whips, the crown, My Flesh they will tear
the evils of men, I must alone bear
Oh Abba! Oh Father! is there no other way?
Must I, Your Son, bear it away?
Yet, Abba! Dear Father, I am Your Son
Thy will, not mine, let it be done.
Mary, my mother, must she at the Cross stand
and watch as each nail pierces feet and hand?
Spare her at least, of what I myself know
that in the hearts of some, My Seed will not grow.
Oh Abba, Oh Father! Must it be she
to see anguish and agony, when they crucify me?
Yet, Abba, Dear Father, I am Your Son
Thy will, not mine, let it be done.
Abba, Father, I am an obedient Son
it is Thy will, not mine, that must be done.
Now rising, I praise You, for Your just decree,
as I turn My Face toward Calvary.

41

Unseen Beauty

Snowflakes falling softly
upon the cold hard ground
whiteness all abounding
so quiet...not a sound
each flake of white's an artwork
made by God's own hand
so many yet none the same
what beauty covers the land
a microscopic masterpiece
that no man can recreate
and yet it will not last
for melting is its fate
I look about in wonder
at every winter scene
and glory in the beauty
that lies hidden there...unseen.

little things

little things of little worth
they may seem to men of earth
but ladies, dragons, butterflies
how much earth on them relies
spots of black on reddish hue
to the rose are friends so true
dragons diving through the air
gnats, mosquitoes are their fare
fluttering aloft on fragile wings
pollen to flowers a butterfly brings
it's little things of little worth
that God uses to beautify earth!

Truth

"Truth? What is truth?" Pilate asked the King of Kings
"How can a man know, when 'truth' is many things?"
When one says "this is real" and another "that is fake"
whom do you believe? of whose 'truth' do you partake?
If truth is really relative and there is no wrong or right
then there is obviously no point in breaking up a fight
just take some time and study from any history book
while keeping your mind set on that 'relativism' hook:
If everything is relative and there is no moral truth
then Lincoln was not murdered at the hand of John Wilkes Booth
and there was no crime at all when Hitler reigned supreme
he just exercised his 'choice' in 'removing' Jews from Germany
and when those hijacked planes hit Towers One and Two
there was no evil there just someone's 'thing' to do.
If truth is really relative, any action that we take
to maim, to kill, to murder, is our own choice to make
but Truth is not relative that's plain enough to see
but still there lies that question: "What is 'truth' to me?"
When Pilate asked that question long ago and far away
he turned and would not listen to what the Lord would say.
Truth is not a thought, something heard, nor something said
no, Truth is a Man Who once rose from the dead
Jesus is the Truth and the way and the life
Who came to earth to save us from bondage, sin and strife.
So let our hearts be open and our minds firm in the fact
that that Truth is there to guide us in every little act.

Palm Song

Here I stand before the Lord
the only God, to be adored
Hosanna in the Highest

Honor praise and glory bring
to the Lord, my God and King
Hosanna in the Highest

Adoration belongs by right
to the Lamb in all His might
Hosanna in the Highest

Son of David, Son of God
O bring Him honor, praise and laud
Hosanna in the Highest

to Father Son and Spirit Three
all praise and glory ever be
Hosanna in the Highest

Holy Face

I saw the Face of God today
although I knew it not
Marred as it was by blood and spit
bruise and livid spot
No beauty in this Countenance
Its comeliness all gone
and yet it was, without a doubt
the Face of God's own Son
What has happened to the Face
of Christ my Sovereign King
to Whom the crowds, just five days past
did sweet "Hosannas" sing?
Oh Jesus, wounded by my sins
when I behold His Face
the tears that stream down from my eyes
both sweet and bitter taste
sweet they are for love of Him
and Love of Him alone,
yet bitter too, for love of me
for my sins He did atone
T'was by His wounds I am set free
my soul cleansed by His grace
So, beaten, bruised, and crowned with Thorns,
how Beauteous His Face!

Judas Kisses

How often do I purse my lips
and offer God a Judas Kiss?
Judas' kiss was one and done
when He betrayed God's only Son
How many more do I provide,
I who claim to be His bride?
When to the world I give a part
of my well-divided heart
and let success inflame my pride,
seeking praise from every side…
When I give in to my desire
for ease and comfort and retire
and waste my time in vain pursuit
of such worthless, worldly fruit…
When I take my eyes off my Groom,
gazing all about the room
and rest them not in my haste
to see, to touch and to taste…
then to my Lover's sinless cheek,
oh so humble and so meek
I press my dirty, defiled lips
and give to Him a Judas Kiss
But when I see what I have done,
betrayed again God's only Son
then I repent and strike my breast
"Mea Culpa" I confess
I run to Him with arms spread wide
taking refuge in His side
and beg pardon for those lips
that once again have betrayed by kiss
He forgives me, even though
both He and I full well know
that it won't be the last mark I miss
…nor the last Judas Kiss.

Contemplation

Sometimes it seems I'm drifting
upon an endless sea
with white capped waves abounding
as far as eye can see
I guess I should be worried
of being lost at sea
and yet I feel not hurried
but happy, calm, and free
Just what is this ocean
upon which I am adrift
or what concoction or potion
has caused this great uplift?
Something has brought me here
(or actually Someone)
so I have naught to fear
for He is the Risen One
This is the pure Love
this endless ocean of bliss
that comes from heaven above
in my Lover's tender Kiss

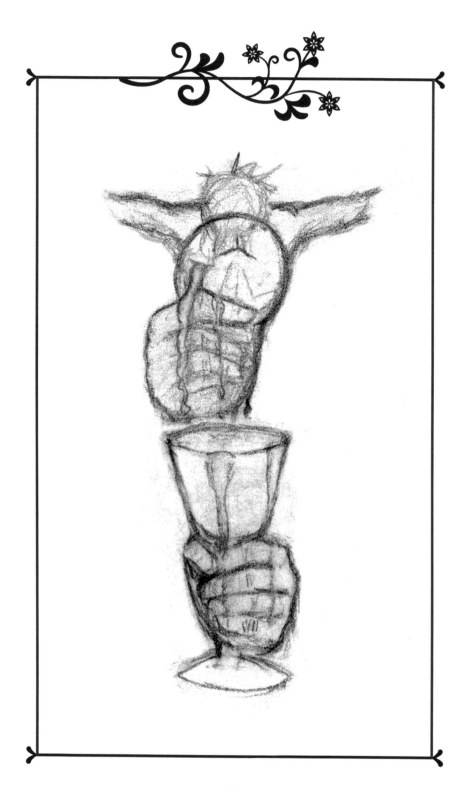

The Embrace

Wrap Your strong arms round me
hide my frailty with Your grace
let Your Love surround me
secure in Your embrace
Oh my Love I adore You
my Savior and my King
I faint for love in Your arms
and my heart cannot but sing
Drunk on Your Blood like wine
You inebriate my soul
and Your Body, my Daily Bread
fills its God-Shaped Hole
O Lover of my Soul
let me die in this Embrace
that when I awake in Heaven
I may rejoice at the sight of Your Face!

Garments of Jesus

Water, flour: mix at high power
cold jugs: seven, just wheat, no leaven
we mix the breads which soon will be
the garments of Jesus, just wait and see!

Water, wheat: pour on heat
steam hiss, try not to miss
we bake the breads which soon will be
the garments of Jesus, just wait and see!

Mist, damp, into stable tramp
feel, wet are they ready yet
we dampen the breads which soon will be
the garments of Jesus, just wait and see!

sheet slides in hosts fill bin
bang, pow! here they come now!
we cut the breads which soon will be
the garments of Jesus, just wait and see!

Eight cuts or more, into boxes pour
turn off light dry overnight
we dry the breads which soon will be
the garments of Jesus, just wait and see!

Shake, shake, watch for breaks
pour, seal, "Prayerfully" peel
we bag the breads which soon will be
the garments of Jesus, just wait and see!

Pack, tape, no sound make
label, weigh, send out Friday
we ship the breads which soon will be
the garments of Jesus, just wait and see!

Hymns sing, offertory bring
bread, wine, almost time
we offer the breads which soon will be
the garments of Jesus, just wait and see!

Listen! Priest: Sacrificial Feast
Word said, no longer bread
God makes the gifts forever be
the Garments of Jesus, now do you see?

The Dilemma

I kick the goad
and buck the load
yet still I'm given more
I will not write
the urge I fight
but the words come to the fore
When I find
that words, not mine
come, unbidden, to preach
my tongue I bite
but lose the fight
and my lips burst into speech
Poetry, art
flow from my heart
causing both pleasure and pain
as misplaced praise
of beauteous phrase
makes a loss out of gain
within my heart
there is a part
that craves the praise I hear
yet stronger still
is Thy will
that tells me not to fear
the words are Thine
they are not mine
that's clear enough to see
and so I sing
and praise I bring
with words that come from Thee

Trinity

Unfathomable mystery
Trinity in Unity
God is Father, Spirit, Son
Yet, undivided, God is One
His is Power, Glory, Might
Who formed the stars, the moon, the night
He the Lamb Who once was slain
Whose Blood cleansed man of every stain
He the Spirit, Bond of Love
Who came from Heav'n as Wild White Dove
God is Father, God is Son
God is Spirit, Three-in-One
All Glory Laud and Jubilee
be to He, the One-in-Three

Holy Souls

Many a time I've heard it said
"Why would anyone pray for the dead?
aren't they in heaven, free from pain?
It's a wasted prayer! you should be ashamed!"
Truth be told I once thought so too
I believed then as they now do
but now I know and now I pray
for those poor souls who in purgatory stay
People don't know, they don't understand
that when we die and before the Lord we stand
He is pure light and in His brightness we see
all the dirt, all the stains from when we chose "me"
because we want to be pure and free from stain
we choose to be purged, we accept the pain
that comes from the longing to see His face
once we are cleansed, purified by Grace.
Since now the dead cannot for themselves pray
they are not able to shorten their stay
so when we pray to lessen their time
they gratefully accept the shortened line
they return the favor and keep us in mind
and their prayers for us we will, one day, find
were just what we needed that extra grace
while still on earth, to quicken our pace
So, Eternal rest grant to them O' Lord
that soon by them in glory You may be adored!

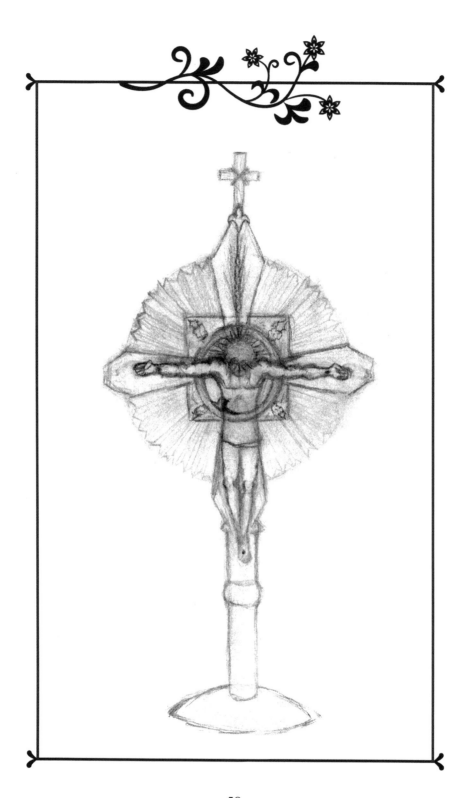

58

Adoration

All colors fade
and turn to gray
around the disc of white
my senses dim
I enter in
although I try to fight
can it be
that what I see
before me here and now
is real and true
…is really You…
this I know somehow
Though I know
that it is so
still I wonder why
from heart of tin
so full of sin
away you do not fly
If I look away
let my eyes stray
to side…above…below
and break the Gaze
the haze then fades
and there and then I know
that I truly see
naught but He
to Whom I am espoused
in the Disc of White
in Monstrance bright
my Beloved, my God, my Spouse

Are You Really Who You Say You Are?

Are you really Who You say You are?
the God Who made the morning star…

He Who fashioned man from clay…
then rested on that seventh day…

are you the king of all that is…
even that which man thinks is his…

are you the God of earth and heaven…
O' little host of bread unleavened?

…Sometimes I wonder if it's true...
…is it really, truly You?…

"Yes, O' little bride of mine
yes, I am the Lord divine

I breathed life that fateful day
into faulty, earthen clay

and on the next I rest My head
in My little manger bed

I am King of all that is
I own all man thinks is his

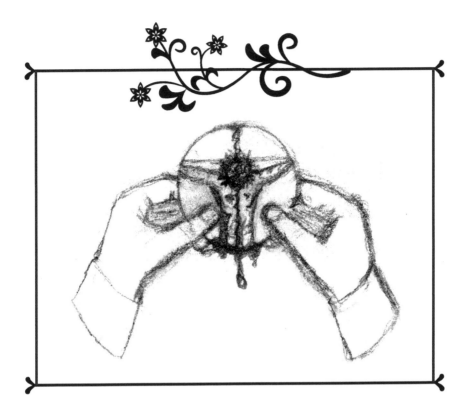

Yes, I made the Morning Star
and I made you the way you are

I made you loving, kind and sweet
and gave to you My Flesh to eat

I made you to question, doubt and think
and gave to you My Blood to drink

Though you doubt, know this is true
I'm the One who made you "you"

Martha, Martha

Look at her just sitting there
gazing at Him with awe-filled stare
lost in time, alone in space
She seems lost within His face
I need her help, why can't she see?
I'd sit too, if I were free
but I've much serving and cooking to do
She should be helping! Lord, tell her to!
"Martha, Martha." Jesus replies,
with love in His Heart, His voice, His eyes
Mary has chosen the far better part
and loves Him with undivided heart.
She sits and she listens to His sonorous voice
I too must listen, and make a choice
Martha or Mary, which shall I be?
Is it work or prayer that sets my soul free?
Sometimes it seems as if I'm pulled one way:
to work like St. Martha, or like Mary pray
for work is a needed, necessary task
but it can be pleasurable, if it makes the time pass
yet, though work can be fun, an enjoyable thing
it truly is prayer that makes my heart sing
Though it may seem a contradiction in terms
it's from both Martha and Mary that a Nun's path she learns
For both followed Jesus, each in her own way
and Martha has her own saintly feast day.
So, Mary and Martha please pray much for me
that beside you in Heaven I may one day be.

Smells and Bells

the Tinkling sound of the ringing of bells
the books and the candles and all of the smells
the swinging gold censer and high-chanted song
all proclaim of God's coming, that it shan't be long
the Scriptures are opened and the Word is read
The Gospel proclaimed and the homily said
bread is then offered and with it the wine
of our hearts and our lives, they are the sign
we join angel chorus, so beautifully lush
then silence falls in supernatural hush
time is forgotten as we draw near to the Cross
When for us all God's life was lost
the Moment passes swiftly, too soon it is done
and where once was bread, now lies God the Son
wine, now His Blood, His Body the Bread
upon which our souls daily are fed
every day, every moment, at every Mass
God comes to man bodily and breaks our fast

Song of the Lictor

The whips that cracked across His back
held by hands so strong
the thorns that mocked the tattered frock
jests of an evil throng
the nails that pierced with pain so fierce
the Cross raised for all to see
all meant to bring pain to the King
were caused, oh Lord, by me
my wicked deeds bore the seeds
of the thorns that brought Him pain
every sinful act plowed His back
furrows of blood new lain
each evil thought a new thread bought
of scarlet for His robe
and by my lust and acts unjust
its cloth I weaved and wove
every blasphemous word each curse he heard
were uttered by my lips
it t'was my wrath that brought the bath
that to the cobbles drips
bound by my lies and broken ties
I lead Him to His Death
I nailed Him high, left Him to die
and waited for His last breath
was then I heard Him speak that word
that I knew was meant for me
"Father forgive… my life I give"
He died to set me free.

Open Eyes

Man, O Lord, can be so blind
And pass by beauty you've left behind
Like drops of dew on blades of grass
Sparkling like shards of broken glass
Like "Johnny-jump-ups" and moths of blue
That leap like my heart leaps up to You
A bee that drinks from a clover flower
The shadows that shift from hour to hour
The subtle strength of spider silk
A new fawn drinking mother's milk
These insignificant, so small things
Such love, such joy, to my heart brings
So much beauty to see and hear
Yet missed by many, this I fear
Open their eyes, Lord, that they may see
All the little wonders You show to me!

Cross-Road

I stand here at the Cross-road
as He bears His heavy Cross-load
and calls to me to follow
and join Him on the way

Will I take that highway
the narrow, not the wide way
and carry my own cross load
close by Him always?

or will I not that way go
but wander through the hedgerow
searching for that other way
which many sinners take?

I must now a choice make
knowing what is at stake
to follow or to leave Him
which way shall I go?

I choose to take the Cross Road
and with my little cross load
I walk with him who calls me
and follow Him on the Way.

If one truly be wise
She cannot choose but likewise
and follow her Beloved
Who loves her as His Bride!

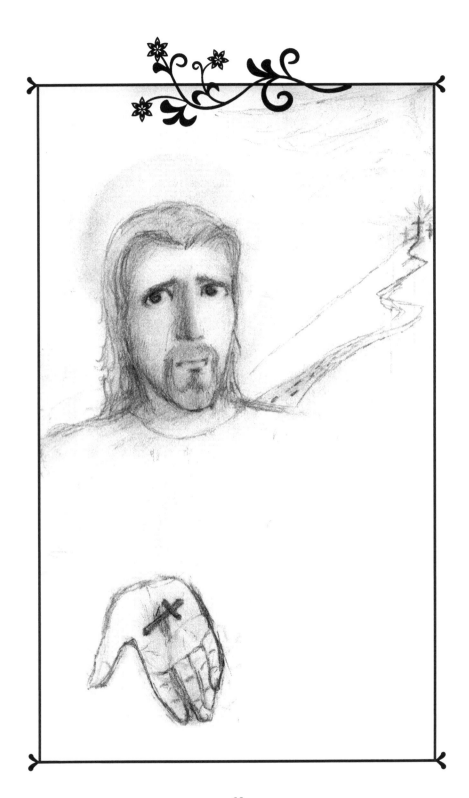

69

Splinters

Your Body bruised and broken
Your Limbs nailed to a tree
Your Blood gushed forth in torrents
to save little sinful me

So why is it that I doubt you?
Why is it I despair?
Is this splinter of a cross
more cross than I can bear?

You loved me into being
You breathed in me new life
You saved me from my bondage
to sorrow, sin and strife

Yet still my heart it wavers
I wander to and fro
though I know Your plan for me
I do not that way go

Lord I beg you answer
yet listen to You not
how than shall I learn
to become what I am not?

My little splinter of a cross
too heavy for me alone
yet I know you're by my side
bearing for me your own

Lord I am so sorry
my heart is full of grief
I fear I'm more a sinner
than Dismas the Good Thief

Just as he stole heaven
may I Your strength steal
that my wounded, broken soul
may by Your love be healed.

The Passionist

Oh Jesus lover
of my soul;
my heart's one
and only goal!

What is it that I
am waiting for,
if not for You,
O God adored?

In the Garden,
at Foot of the Cross
watching, waiting,
as Life is lost.

Waiting in
the dark of night,
waiting still
at dawn's first light.

I wait and watch
and always pray
and by the Cross
forever stay.

Psalmody

the little bell has rung
the Office has begun
the Psalms of David sung
in praise of God.

Seven times each day
we gather here to pray
to sanctify the day
and bring Him laud.

Side by side we praise
by turn our voices raise
singing each beauteous phrase
back and forth, to and fro.

Our hearts to Him we bring
our Savior and our King
with full voice we sing
the hymns of long ago.

one of our number leads
From the Scriptures reads
as our souls He feeds
with Words from Heaven sent.

we well understand
we hear the word of man
guided by God's hand
with Spirit that He lent.

May this Liturgy of ours
that we sing at all the Hours
fill these hearts of ours
with unbounded love.

May God on us bestow
in this way of which we know,
to walk this earth below
yet live in heaven above.

Afterword: If I Knew Then...

"If only I knew then
what I know now"
wistful people often say
but if I knew then
what I know now
I wouldn't be here today
living life
a day at a time
as if each were my last
I am so grateful
to my God
for all the days now past
He kept me safe
from so much harm
kept my intentions pure
through all the heartache
all the pain
I rested in Him secure
O Lord,
How can I thank You
for all you've done for me:
the little bit
that I know now
and all I do not see?
In thanksgiving
for what I know
may I always be true
and live each moment
of my life
O Lord, my Love, for You!

Made in the USA
Middletown, DE
27 November 2022

16146303R00046